IN YOUR OWN TIME

IN YOUR OWN TIME:

THE NORTHERN POETRY WORKSHOP ANTHOLOGY

EDITED BY GERRY WARDLE
FOREWORD BY SEAN O'BRIEN

Shoestring Press

Printed by imprintdigital
Upton Pyne, Exeter
www.imprintdigital.net

Typeset by narrator
www.narrator.me.uk
enquiries@ narrator.me.uk

Published by Shoestring Press
19 Devonshire Avenue, Beeston, Nottingham, NG9 1BS
(0115) 925 1827
www.shoestringpress.co.uk

First published 2012
© Copyright: Peter Armstrong, Peter Bennet, Colette Bryce, Alistair Elliot, Helen Farish, Paul Farley, W N Herbert, Joan Hewitt, Joan Johnston, Michael McCarthy, Sean O'Brien, Jacob Polley, Katharine Towers, Tony Williams
The moral rights of the authors have been asserted.
ISBN 978 1 907356 44 5

ACKNOWLEDGEMENTS

Poems in this anthology have appeared in the following publications: *Cimarron Review, Oxford Magazine, Poetry London, PN Review, Poetry Review, Qualm, Southlight, The North, The Rialto, TLS*.

Peter Bennet's 'The Stitchers' from *The Glass Swarm* (2008) and 'The Chrysalis', 'Spraunce', and 'Unity in the Englischer Garten' from *The Game of Bear* (2011) are reprinted by permission of Flambard Press.

Colette Bryce's poems are from *Self-Portrait in the Dark* (2008) and are reprinted by permission of Picador, an imprint of Pan Macmillan, London.

Paul Farley's poems are from *Tramp in Flames* (2006) and are reprinted by permission of Picador, an imprint of Pan Macmillan, London.

W N Herbert's 'A Heart of Trees' and 'Jacobite's Ladder' from *The Laurelude* (1998) and 'For Andrew Waterhouse' from *Bad Shaman Blues* (2006) are reprinted by permission of Bloodaxe Books; 'Comrade Bear' and 'Metaphor for Malchik' from *Three Men on the Metro* (2009) by permission of Five Leaves Poetry.

Joan Hewitt's 'The Maestro' from *Missing the Eclipse* (2008) is reprinted by permission of Cinammon Press.

Joan Johnston's 'Fathers of the Early 50s' from *Orange for the Sun* (2005) is reprinted by permission of Dog Eater Press; 'A Blue Plaque - above a Front Door', 'Pol in her Coffin', 'The Old Bus Shelter', 'The Burning Map' from *The Daredevil: Scenes from a Bigamist Marriage... and other poems* (2011) are reprinted by permission of Red Squirrel Press.

Michael McCarthy's 'The Long Road to London', 'The Fields', 'Cold Hill Pond', 'Beachcombing' from *At the Races* (2009) are reprinted by permission of Smith/Doorstop Books.

Sean O'Brien's 'Reading Stevens in the Bath' from *Cousin Coat: Selected Poems 1976-2001* (2002), 'Indian Summer' from *Downriver* (2001), 'Blizzard' from *The Drowned Book* (2007) and 'Elegy' from *November* (2011) are reprinted by permission of Picador, an imprint of Pan Macmillan, London.

Jacob Polley's 'Man' from *The Brink* (2003) and 'The Byre' from *Little Gods* (2006) are reprinted by permission of Picador, an imprint of Pan Macmillan, London.

Katharine Towers' 'The Art of Fugue' and 'Pianola' from *The Floating Man* (2010) are reprinted by permission of Picador, an imprint of Pan Macmillan, London.

Tony Williams' 'Poem for Tuesday', 'Late Schoolboys' and 'The Corner of Arundel Lane and Charles Street' from *The Corner of Arundel Lane and Charles Street* (2009) are reprinted by permission of Salt Publishing.

CONTENTS

FOREWORD

The Northern Poetry Workshop dates back to my time as Northern Arts Literary Fellow from 1992-94, when I held an initial meeting at the Literary and Philosophical Society Library in Newcastle in order to discover whether there would be any interest in beginning a group for poets who had published books or were shortly to do so. The result has proved far more durable than I imagined. 2012 will mark the Northern Poetry Workshop's twentieth year of monthly meetings. This anthology celebrates its longevity and vigour.

Membership is by invitation. The group's approach is familiar and straightforward. The poet listens to a discussion of his/her poem and is then invited to respond to the group's observations. The tone is serious but respectful and the occasion is convivial. As the usual chair of the meetings, I remain excited by the evidence of the growth and development of the poets' work, by the overall calibre of the participants, and by the quality of attention, and the humour, that people bring to our discussions. The process seems to answer to a wish for thoughtful comment on matters of technique and for a sense of common imaginative endeavour.

Naturally the membership has changed over time, though there are still survivors from the earliest days of the group. Some of the current participants travel considerable distances to attend. We owe a particular debt to Joan Hewitt for her warm hospitality over many years.

The late Andrew Waterhouse (1958-2001) had begun to attend the workshop not long before his tragic early death. It is to this gifted and much-missed poet that this anthology is affectionately dedicated.

Sean O'Brien

PETER ARMSTRONG

AN EXPIATION

You caught one final glimpse of him
hungover on a northbound train
examining his conscience in lieu of memory.

At Grantham seen to beg for drink;
by York was screaming for a priest,
for penances as pure as they were terrible.

His secretary waited hours
and then went home. The next of kin
was unavailable. His flat was perfect and unvisited.

Rumour had him last at Thurso
waving at who'd ever pause
tickets for the non-existent line

beyond Dounray into the clean
and purging rain; chanting with
a visionary lilt the station's names

from Farr, Coldbackie, Tongue
to the inevitable terminus, Cape Wrath.

NEHWON

If it were the case that you had woken
stranded where the trains had given over
waiting in the rain beside the river,
platforms gone to blackberry and bracken;

crossing by the bridge above the weir
(strung between an always and the never)
surely you would find beyond the river
villages of institute and spire

where, for all the labours of the weather
chiselling exactly and forever
sliver after sliver after sliver,
time had bound its aggregates together.

Dialects that come to the air untroubled
clear above the quarrels of the weir
mark you as the only stranger here
instantly, and place you with the fabled

denizens of any other era.
Everything is running to its schema:
manners, newsprint, adverts, roadsigns, grammar;
all that keeps its word to pay the bearer

where the myth that nothing lasts forever
bows before the civil weight of detail.
Had you been found shivering and foetal
washed up with the wrack beside the river,

how long you had slept is not the matter
nor that you are aged or an infant:
strangers take your hand and for the moment
bid you to attend to how the water

trundles by with neither past nor future;
visit in their gaze a kind of pity
(were you, after all, to choose a city:
bright, inconstant, altogether other).

MIRFIELD

i.m. Aelred Stubbs, CR

While we slept
the rain ticked at the glass
like the ghost of Bede's sparrow
less for shelter than
to bring from the kindly dead
their travellers' tales of Purgatory.
Waking to the blue-grey dusk,
to the cowled brethren tacking over
the soaked lawns' winter reaches
(and whether from hope or hope's ending,
whether from the body's knowledge
or the reticence of truth)
we found ourselves without a word,
the garden another continent,
the road home a page of sleet
we, both of us, refrained from reading.

MULLAGHNADREESRUHAN AFTER RAIN

for Barney Devine

Ireland, especially in the west, is an amphibious kind of land; if you want to probe effectively into its corners, some sort of amphibious costume becomes necessary

                                                          R.L.Praeger, *The Way That I Went*

To prove utter indifference to moisture, the writer walked into the river and sat down on a submerged stone and began to eat lunch

                                          R.M.Barrington, *vol. xvii, The Irish Naturalist, 1908*

I fasted on Guinness and Mackerel
before coming to baptism in a Bluestacks downpour
and here declare: myself absurdly cleansed;
the ur-philosopher correct
who held the One to be water.

Robert Lloyd Praeger, be my guide:
the rain has turned to sphagnum moss;
the moss has turned to river;
the river so forgotten itself
as to fold into its lover.

And that convenient fiction, self
(that edge against which I
have scratched my ogham narrative)
has rubbed away against the kiss of gneiss,
against the light off Donegal bay,
against a foreign tongue
you'd fancied nestled in the blood.

But that's enough:
now plodge down through your element
that gathers up all opposites
into its solving flux;
and wraps the body in its transparent shroud
and leaves the soul in rags.

BETWEEN GREENHEAD AND SEWINGSHIELDS

You never meant to come to this
emblem of the distances,
nor understood how mind could lie
stripped of its contingency.
You know the kind of road I mean:
Zeno's proof embodied in
this tarmac and unbroken line
by which you near, though never reach,
the blind crest of the moon-drawn ridge.

You'll flick the headlights up to full,
give yourself to that parable
of the further edge, where, for good or ill,
the field of vision's infinite
as the nothing you illuminate.
The guide geography's written for your heart
has brought you to your heart's desire,
neither destination nor detour
but, friend, indubitably here.

Soon, you will pull over,
turn the lights and engine off,
and step without a thought onto the verge,
where, lacking name or face or age,
we'll leave you to, or not, or past, yourself,
the propositions night dissolves,
that sometime fellow-traveller, belief.
Goodnight. Good luck. God help you, friend,
world without (I mean it) end.

PETER BENNET

AUGENLICHT

The place we've come to leans against the sky
and dreams the moon. A midden steams.
We start a hare. We are alive.

The roads we took were intricate
and bad. Though fearful we were not deterred.
A pale girl gathers shadows from the track.

She whispers an irrevocable word
of which no meaning will survive.
She is inured to working late.

The night is old. Her one bright eye
fades from our way. She's what she seems.
She moves the oceans when she turns her back.

THE CHRYSALIS

She had been childless until late one day
when all sides of the house were casting shadow
projected by the sinking sun
or by the rising moon. Only the stone
flags of the terrace glowed, and the chrysalis
that lay there good as gold and lovable,
breathing like blossom in the dark
and half a metre long. She took it in.
Next morning as red insects swarmed
against the windows and a trout
on the cold slab in the pantry rolled its eye
she placed it on the broad lip of the fountain
despite the thin east wind and pointed out
the steeple on the hill among the trees
although of course it could not see.
It slept upon her lap that afternoon
when she had company to hear the priest
discuss the evidence for Noah's Ark
but no one noticed it. It didn't show
itself in that way ever. But it grew
and then transmogrified and flew away,
iridescent and immense, so beautiful
it left her all a-flutter and transformed
back into a child herself, quick as a lark,
on cherub's wings above her vacant pew.

SPRAUNCE

The bald rock got in at the beginning,
a mirage so to speak, though not like those
we fell for in the desert, spinning

tanks and trucks from heat waves. I suppose
her cigarette smoke was the haze
that veiled it in the estuary. Her clothes

came off. She made me look. A kid in those days,
a lot too young for grown-up girls
to bother with you'd think. You'd be amazed.

Her tongue and fingers, crimped blonde curls
all over me. That mewing sound.
Perhaps that's why I mixed up girls and gulls.

Just over there it happened, in the dunes.
I had to help her button up her dress.
She said she'd send her brother round

to belt me if I blabbed. I thought the fuss
she made would get her pregnant and she'd blame me.
The smell of female sweat still makes me queasy.

I didn't understand that she was happy
doing that noise, like crying only sharper.
After school it was the army.

Dodging Rommel. Then the kind of caper –
accounts and such – that's no great shakes but steady.
Computers came and that was time to scarper.

It's strange how many women have been ready
to flash the go-ahead as bold as brass.
And married women. Once a titled lady.

I'd never tell them and they'd never guess
the reason why I fobbed them off.
I think the bald rock saved me, more or less,

from going barmy with the shell-shock stuff,
explosions, guts and beaks, and finger-ends.
Thank God it's calmed down now. I've had enough.

Most summer nights I raise a few tall gins –
out on the front lawn by the patch of pampas –
to all consenting lovers in the dunes

and silt and salt, all seas and rivers.
Although the medics have me down for cancer
it's still the thought of sex that gives me shivers.

I take the treatment, look quite spraunce.
Who knows, maybe reprieve is on the cards.
I'll settle for a 50/50 chance

and the sea view from my bungalow towards
the old bald rock there in his wig of birds.

THE STITCHERS

The consequence of poetry is shame

Douglas Dunn

What they're embroidering is us, full pelt
through clutching memory, clump after clump,
until each likeness stumbles, and its rump,
in artful needlework, yields to the grip

of grinning anthropophagi.
We're in a version of the Feast of Guilt,
where consequences eat intention,
chewing fingers, howking out an eye,

then relishing the succulence
of butchered limb and bloody stump.
They'll stitch us into grief until we die,
and yet the teeth that gnaw and rip

at silk or corpse meat are our own.
The only exit is impenitence,
or one small window in the word *good-bye*
through which we would be mad to jump.

UNITY IN THE ENGLISCHER GARTEN

She went to Parteitagen as to Mass
and still prays to the Führer, but in vain.
She let the dear storms commandeer a flat
On Agnesstrasse. When the Jews who own
nothing now but old age and their bags had gone
she turned her future in the lock.
She dreams that lava-heaps and cinder-cones
rise from hot sand when she tries to run
and then veiled women in a great black car
as dawn comes crush her in a Swinbrook lane.
Now rooks with silver swastikas convene
mock parliaments among the trees
beside the Haus der Kunst. The day is warm
and she is beautiful. She sees
across the park the Isar fuss
among its channels in an English manner
with swarming khaki backwaters. Her brain
must calculate her worth. The world's at war.
The British Consulate is off the phone.
There's no one left to play with or to shock.
A green bench shimmers in the sun.
Wearing her crimped hair like a hat
she sits there to relax and points the gun
against her blank cherubic face.
She is a kind of saint. We need not care
nor spare the time to think of her again.

COLETTE BRYCE

A SPIDER

I trapped a spider in a glass,
a fine-blown wineglass.
It shut around him, silently.
He stood still, a small wheel
of intricate suspension, cap
at the hub of his eight spokes,
inked eyes on stalks; alert,
sensing a difference.
I meant to let him go
but still he taps against the glass
all Marcel Marceau
in *the wall that is there but not there*,
a circumstance I know.

SELF-PORTRAIT IN A BROKEN WING-MIRROR

The lens has popped from its case,
minutely cracked and yet intact, tilted
where it stopped against a rock on the tarmac.
And this could be Selkirk, washed up on a beach,
in prone position surveying the sweep
of his future sanctuary, or prison.

But no, that's me, a cubist depiction: my ear,
its swirl and ridge of pearly cartilage,
peachy lobe and indent of a piercing
not jewelled for years. I punctured that
with a nerve of steel at fifteen in a bolted
room. It was Hallowe'en. I had no fear.

The ear is parted neatly from the head
by breaks in the glass, a weird mosaic
or logic puzzle for the brain to fix.
The eyebrow, stepped in sections, stops
then starts again, recognisably mine.
The nose, at an intersection of cracks,

is all but lost except for the small sculpted
cave of a shadowy nostril. The eye
is locked on itself, the never-easy gaze
of the portraitist, the hood half open,
the hub of the pupil encircled with green
and a ring of flame. I have make-up on,

a smudging of pencil, brushed black lashes.
I'd swear the face looks younger than before,
the skin sheer, the fine wires of laughter
disappeared without the animation.
The lips are slack, pink, segmented;
a slight gravitational pull towards the earth

gives the upper one a sort of Elvis curl.
The same effect has made the cheek more full.
I have never been so still. A beautiful day
and not another car for what seems like hours.
Also in the glass, bisected, out of focus,
a streamer of road and a third of sky.

Presently, I will attempt to move,
attempt to arise in a shower of diamonds,
but first I must finish this childish contest
where one must stare the other out, not look
away, like a painting in a gallery, where
only the blink of an eye might restart time.

NATURE WALK

If only my bag had been large enough,
I would have brought the lonely men in parked cars
by the river. I would have brought the woman
dabbing kohl tears with the heel
of her hand. I might have brought the ancient couple
who read each word on the YOU ARE HERE
board, then turned and ambled on, heads
a little upward-tilted, showing
an interest in everything.

I would have brought the coping-stone
from the twelfth pier of the original bridge, and the 4:06
from elsewhere, curving (glittering) carefully across.
and all the busy people on it; all their coats
and phones and wallets. I might
have brought the restless gulls that dropped
like paper boats on the water. And the burger van,
the girl inside with greasy hair,
her quite unsolvable crossword.

And put them all on my nature table,
and fashioned little cardboard signs:
a small display that would speak in a way
about loneliness and life spans, parked cars and rivers.

I brought some bark, and a couple of conkers,
one still half-encased in its skin like an eye.

SEVEN IN BED

(Louise Bourgeois)

A muddle of thick limbs like a knot
of sausages in a butcher's window.
It is night here, they are trying to sleep.
It is morning. They are awakening, yawning.
Pink as the meat on a sheet of white,
they are seven in bed, and nothing
is quite what it seems. Two-headed,
Janus-faced, are they clinging to each other
or trying to escape? Their stitched seams
have a rawness, surgical. Long groans
attest to a struggle. Prisoners.
They are like wrestlers in a scrum.
Is it love? Do they love each other?

ONCE

Some words you may use only once.
Repeat them to some newer heart
and all your accuracy is gone.
                    Denise Riley

Sweetheart, darling. Years on,
how the old terms fail;
words that we loved with, once.

Older, on our second chance,
we stand, faltering hearts
in hands, inaccurate

and passionate, in love's
late, unfurnished rooms,
full of the words we cannot use;

and drive home, the same
streets, drop through the gears
to steer around the gone

words, the known
words, the beautiful outworn
words, those we may use only once,
all our accuracy gone.

ALISTAIR ELLIOT

THE ROAST PIG – AUGUST 24, AD 410

All of us had looked forward to that meal,
my husband, and some senators, and I.
My maid told me the pig came from Calabria,
and would be butchered in the afternoon
by her first lover, Marius, in the kitchen.
It turned out we would only get a taste
(the smell was in the lower rooms for hours)
as we'd barely started eating when the prefect
of the praetorian guard came shouting down
the marble corridor saying Alaric
was in the city. He had been let in
by the old keeper of the Porta Salaria
and all his troops were making for the palace.
Later I heard that Alaric was pleased
to find the carved pork on the golden plates,
and he and his lieutenants ate it all.
It seemed that Rome was welcoming his Goths...
Nevertheless, they pillaged Rome for days.
I sometimes wonder if he took the plates,
and that's the treasure that they say is buried
beside him in the river bed, not far
from where the pig we shared was born and raised.

BUXTEHUDE'S DAUGHTER

Father would say I thought Orlando Lasso
Was an epic on the old age of a hero –
He teased me horribly. But he also tried
To leave me safe and settled when he died,
Offering my hand in marriage to the best
Who came to take his seat – the musical test,
Then me, the princess of this fairy tale.
That's what he thought. To me, I was for sale
Like fading goods in a window, in our house
Sewing, to show I'd make a model spouse.

When Handel came, he found me elderly.
He was eighteen and I was twenty-eight –
The sad arithmetic of too soon, too late...
I wonder if he ever thinks of me
At night, in London. He liked my soup that day.
Strange to know someone famous far away.

Then young Bach came. He was so keen to learn
He overstayed, and I began to burn
Like a ripe candle in my room alone
Along the corridor. Which he must have known.
Father and he became so close. He knew
The parent's hope – but never called me Du.
Three months I was for sale and was not bought.

Though absent in the wood of musical thought
He must have seen my shape, at meals, because
Unwittingly I fired him for his cousin,
The young and merry one who sang.

                                    And then
Father no longer walked, but flew to heaven.
I still kept house, now for his deputy.
They offered him the job and he took me,

That autumn. So I moved into the bed
Where I was born, and gave my maidenhead
In the same place - where I expect to die.

We have a cat and dog. Johann and I
Named them from operas he composed before
We met: Medea, the Euripidean whore,
And Alaric, the Gothic king. Johann
Christian Schieferdecker ist mein Mann,
Natürlich jünger - just four years, this time.
And do you ask if we had children? Nein.

I made the Elders give Johann more pay:
Organists wear their trouser-seats away -
All that sliding along the bench, you know.
When he plays Bach, he sweats a bit. I glow.

FLORIDA – JANUARY 1941

Mostly we walked from the cottage to the beach.
My sisters and Miss Love went round the lake;
I rowed across. The oars would sometimes bump
On coconuts with soft beards of water plants.
Each time I thought I'd hit a water beast,
And speeded up – but it was just a nut
Rolling, beheaded, in the dotted lane,
That long neat wake. My excellent rowing-teacher
Was an imaginary alligator.

The drive bent round and met the road; we crossed,
Following a dirt track through dry cabbage-palms
To The Beach House. Beyond the coral reef
The Atlantic opened: over there was home,
Out past the Gulf Stream, where a tanker burned
And the oil of war slid in towards the beach.

Portuguese men-o'-war lay on the sand,
Poisonous barrage-balloons. I used to think
If I rowed out so far, I could stop rowing:
The Stream, uncoiling from the Spanish Main,
Would carry us on its bluer warmer waters
North to Cape Hatteras, on to Nova Scotia –
Picking our way among the submarines,
We'd come to the old Scotland, to the loch
So often mentioned in our father's letters
And the little islands opposite Glencoul,
A beach covered with snow, where the Big Stag
Led down the hinds to feed on bladderwrack,
Or the family's own green beans, in a hard winter.

A GARRISON INSPECTION IN RAVENNA

Apollo, if I ever made a song
That pleased you or that made you sing along,
I beg you, help me now. I must receive
The Emperor who - you know - does not believe
In you or your companions in the sky,
But someone we refer to (secretly)
As the Dead Fish.
                And there are other things
I must not think. So many of us here
Have memories, half-memories we fear,
Of what we did when we were young and free
On leave in Syria, days of liberty,
And nights of even more. We can't recall
The names, but something much more personal
From many bodies, details of a self...

I remember fingering the little breast
Of a tavern virgin. Probably a man,
Now that I think of it.
                I recall a tassel
Swung on a nipple like a thirsty comet
And waking up in the morning smeared with vomit,
Not knowing how I got back to my bunk.

My member has some memories of its own
Stowed among mine. Could they be shared by one
Who later had spectacular success?
What am I going to say if the Empress
Who in her youth readily doffed her clothes
Remembers me for giving her a dose?

Apollo help me! I can't ask the Fish!

OWNING TREES

They called their elm-trees Leonard and Virginia.
It was a solid version of their marriage.
She wrote in front of them; they waved their arms
in sympathy. One of the trees blew down;
the other caught a Dutch disease and died.

We also have two trees, great blossomers –
myrobalan plums is what we think they are –
and assigned them to our sons, but now, years later,
none of us four remembers which is which.
The birds recall they nested on the left,

and insects, who distinguish the two nectars,
can recognise their home from down the street,
how the leaves smell, a light scratch on the bark
made by the elegant cat across the road.
But we cannot remember which is whose.

The names we gave are falling off. The names
Linnaeus and Anon attached so well
will follow: elm, myrobalan, plum and hawthorn,
sapiens, merula, pipiens, canorus,
and all the nouns of Adam – blown away.

This is our loss; the living will not mind
losing a label that was never there
for them – a word that floated like a thought
between us. And still less will they regret
the namers who abandon here for ever.

HELEN FARISH

ALLINGTON CROSS

I keep thinking how we wait all year
and possibly longer (because not every summer
contains such days) for such days.

Because when summer is at its very height
its poise is the pause of a church bell suspended
rim-up after its stroke, mouth open.

At Allington Cross the whole landscape
was a bell mouth open, *ah*, the luminous
untrammelled now of it, rim-up and poised:

And paused at the crossroads in the liquefying
high-sky heat I understood the composer
who cycled round and round the square

so as not to miss a note of the broadcast symphony.

CONCERNING THE LOCATION OF ALEXANDER THE GREAT'S BODY

Even dead, Alexander moves round his city.
A gold sarcophagus opposite the Shrine of the Muses
served for a while, pointing his feet to the sea,
the glitter of whose light he'd swear he could hear
when land-locked, the sound of Macedonia
calling him home.

Melted down, the gold of his sarcophagus became
coins exchanged for this, that or the other;
when newly minted it was as though fishermen
had hauled in a shoal of light, their catch
leaving a matt patch on the metallic surface
of the moneyed sea.

Where next? Some say to a high-walled necropolis
beyond the Suez Canal road, this time a chamber
of marble and centuries of Orthodox wailing,
Greeks being buried as noisily as they lived,
the hearts of mourners filling like sails
yielding to the wind.

Egyptian Antiquities Limited failed
in the 1990s to find him but that doesn't mean he isn't
where Sultan Mohammed Ali said he was,
just up the road from the east-west Canopic way
whose marble colonnades extended as far as
the Gate of the Sun.

Discredited now are the woman and her husband
whose research took the dead Alexander back to Siwa
and the oasis visited once to consult the Oracle.
Setting aside the question of misread inscriptions,
would a man of the sea choose to spend eternity
deep inside a desert dune?

And what about this version of his story?
His bones in a barrel of salt pork, smuggled
out of Alexandria at dead of night by Venetians
convinced, in 981, their cargo was Saint Mark.
Has he been within spume-distance of the Adriatic
ever since, a saint by mistake?

Oh, to have lived a death the subject of such debate!
When I relocate to Rosley, will the unoiled gate squeak
for my sake?

LITERACY LESSON
Wuthering Heights, Chapter 32

We only learn how life is being lived on that day,
at the two houses, thanks to a cart of oats,
newly reaped oats, which happened to pass
as an observant hostler refreshed Lockwood's horse.

So is it good news or bad for those lives
that the very greenness of the oats
prompted the hostler to put down his pail,
tut-tut and exclaim against Gimmerton folk

late again with their harvest – good news or bad
that dreamy Lockwood woke up to where he was?
If close to Gimmerton then close also to the Grange,
a property he rents. Later there'll be a moon,

but with sunlight blowing on the harebell moors
of September 1802, Lockwood detours to find
the Grange's housekeeper enjoying a meditative pipe
on the horse-steps, and a girl of nine or ten knitting.

Even the peaceful curl of blue smoke from the kitchen chimney
is disturbed by the master's change of plan: hot cinders
are raked, fires poked, sheets stretched and scorched,
that quiet courtyard hour in the late sun lost.

Does it make the three-months-dead Heathcliff live again,
the fact that Lockwood, his tenant, now walks
the stony by-road that branches off to Wuthering Heights
expecting to pay his landlord any monies owing?

It was noon when the cart of oats passed. Moonrise now
as Lockwood nears Wuthering Heights, doors and windows
open to the warmth, the smell of wallflowers and stocks.
Not because of the oats, but of their very greenness

the private idling moments of another housekeeper
are interrupted – Nelly Dean loves on such nights
to sit singing on the threshold, moths the colour
of summer butter fluttering. But in the living room,

Catherine and Hareton, playing teacher and pupil,
turn their page undisturbed. Lockwood must let them run,
once their work is done, across the moors to the end
the book has longed for and which Hareton now can read.

THE MONKEY CLOCK

The monkey's eyes go right, go left.
See the sloping flag floor, the range,
Willie Mackereth on his chair, knees to chin.
See George Mackereth, a white cat on his lap,
The World at One at his elbow.

See the bureau, the day's business,
1972's calendar on March.
Here's Hilda Benn with bread and butter,
a tea pot in its cosy. Set them down.
The rain that has decided to fall

on that day at that time is falling.
One moment I see you, says the monkey,
one moment I don't. Where is he,
in his Victorian jacket and tie,
where is he and what does he see now?

Eyes right, eyes left at the window –
Dad's coming to collect his daughters,
hear stories of playing slip-slidey
on the chaise longue in the parlour
behind the back parlour, supervised

by china dogs; how one day George
said the monkey straightened his tie.
The stuffed fox, eyes fixed, told no tales.
Up close we believed we could smell
his lair and hear a beck clattering away.

At the fork in the corridor, Mr Fox,
keeping you in his line of vision,
slowing down time as you head towards him,
the flags moulded to rock, a strip of carpet
to the flags, my young hands to the jampot.

I am returning to the pantry
where sconces moulded to the walls
have stored food for four centuries
of families now dwindled to two
brothers, their housekeeper.

Monkey, turn yourself back.
Let 1972 be on the wall,
let cares be in the bureau,
cats be on laps and let the world
be at one. Let the fox leap

in his case, the tails of china dogs
wag in welcome, let the rain say
I'll fall today. Eyes right,
eyes left. *One moment*
I see you.

RESURRECTION, WIGTON

*Michelangelo requested that his body be buried in Santa Croce so that on Judgement
Day the first thing he'd see would be Brunelleschi's cathedral dome.*

I'd be under the Keswick apple tree
not far from the daffodils
which every spring spell ANNE.

Dad cutting the grass
would be the first thing I'd see.
Don't die again, the first thing I'd say.

Somehow it became everything –
the cobble stone house, the barn,
the ghyll view, the Pennines deciding

on their daily shade of blue, clothes drying
in winds which had names, and the Sycamores
I called Father, Son and Holy Ghost.

And each day we laid innocently
on top of the last dug our names deeper.
Spring will always bring them back

in the distance between the Keswick apple
and the back door, the slight incline,
the bramleys, the old swing swinging

as though I'd just jumped off,
aged ten, my whole life
behind me.

PAUL FARLEY

THE LAPSE

When the cutting edge was a sleight, a trick of time,
we blinked our way through *Jason and the Argonauts*,
thrilled by the stop-motion universe,
its brazen Talos grinding like a Dock Road crane,
and the Hydra's teeth sown into studio soil
by Harryhausen, who got between the frames
like a man who comes in bone dry from a downpour
by stopping the world and snapping out a path
through glassy rods right up to his front door.

Something as simple as Edgerton's milk splash
stilled to an ivory coronet would do it,
keep us quiet for hours as we learned to understand
the howling gale we stood in. Chilled to the core
we gasped as Ursula Andress stepped from the flame
and the unseen British-Pathé make-up department
took down her face, applying gravity with a trowel.
And I'd have to say something was taken from us.

On the dead sheep's seconds-long journey to nothing
with maggots working like a ball of fire,
every now and then a long bone settled awkwardly
like a break in continuity. Like an afternoon
of finding out for ourselves what death smelt like.
Long afternoons. Lying on our backs watching clouds
with the slow Doppler of a plane being bowed across the sky.
Give us back the giant day. Give us back what's ours.

BRUTALIST

Try living in one. Hang washing out to dry
and break its clean lines with your duds and smalls.
Spray tribal names across its subway walls
and crack its flagstones so the weeds can try

their damnedest. That's the way. Fly-tip the lives
you led, out past its edges, on the back field;
sideboards and mangles made sense in the peeled
spud light of the old house but the knives

are out for them now. This cellarless, unatticked
place will shake the rentman off, will throw
open its arms and welcome the White Arrow
delivery fleet which brings the things on tick

from the slush piles of the seasonal catalogues.
The quilt boxes will take up residence
on the tops of white wardrobes, an ambulance
raise blinds, a whole geography of dogs

will make their presence felt. And once a year
on Le Corbusier's birthday, the sun will set
bang on the pre-ordained exact spot
and that is why we put that slab just there.

One by one the shopkeepers will shut
their door for good. A newsagent will draw
the line at buttered steps. The final straw
will fill the fields beyond. Now live in it.

FILLER

This doodle darkening my delegate pack
    on the sixth day of a seven-day conference
is keeping me from screaming. I have the knack
    for honeycombing out the present. Once
I didn't, and the world would turn to filler.
        Not hardnosed economics, like the soldier
        being sent up to the front, or why our butcher
saw fit to scoop sawdust into his mince.

Neither makeweight nor object from the past
    sticking it out from surplus-to-requirements
to value; time sanctifying waste.
    Not superstitious acres farmers grant
        to their crop devil, or a brewer's angels' share.
For me, none of this was strictly filler.
        I saw the use in test-cards and screen-savers.
    Even *Farley, get in goal!* bore fruitful stints.

But never listening to Horace, nor my mother,
eternity turned everything to filler,
our landscapes ground in time to a fine powder,
the bones of Stone Age man, readers and writers,
    the great iron ships, the balance sheets, the sales spikes,
    the last plant standing ancient history,
a sun like blood. Next thing, I'm waving *Goodbye!*
to the hydrogen atom as the seas boil dry,
    which is no way to live. So I take shelter
in the moment's coral, careful not to look
    into the whirlpool of the conference clock.

PHILISTINES

They enter here and leave here through the big doors
    and pass by, unnoticed, though if you watch
any city street your eyes can learn to lock
    onto them. Follow the money. Find your big coat
and get outside: all this looking out the window
    puts daylight between things. Keen as a razor
you see them now: fuzzy-edged, in need of razors
    or loaded down with bags, slamming the doors
of taxis; stood in pairs at shop windows
    absorbed in a new season, keeping watch
from bus shelters, nodding to iPods, coats
    stinking in the rain. A mechanism locks
them outside Wittgenstein and Kant and Locke,
    outside *The Rights of Man* or Occam's Razor;
prevents them slipping Arnold in their coats
    or hearing what's beyond the Frostian door;
admiring *Las Meninas* or *The Night Watch*,
    or writing sestinas in Word for Windows.
Do they see the world we miss, squeegeeing our windows
    or cutting keys to fit our abstract locks?
When she tweezers up the mainspring of a watch
    does it feel like giving birth? When he strops razors
or applies gloss to a freshly sanded door,
    what riptides flood the arm with every stroke and coat?
Their low puns and their proverbs used to coat
    your tongue, but now you pity them at windows
ghostly in plasma light, smoking in door-
    ways, scraping back long bolts, checking locks
half cut on supermarket shiraz or
    sauvignon blanc before turning in. They watch
the clock. Sometimes a boss will tap his watch
    and shake his head, slowly. Poor bastards. Coats
never visit theatre cloakrooms; angry razor-
    burn blooms in call centres without windows

where Post-Its stick like shit to shoes. They'd lock
    horns with the likes of you. Get indoors
where razors glide, where windows hiss tight shut,
    where watches flow, where coats dream on their pegs
and doors lock with a satisfying *click*.

DORMOUSE STRONGHOLD

Over a hundred years we've fortified
our ranges; at the last count just thirty miles
from where we escaped The Collections: while the mink
and grey squirrel are coming soon to a place
near you (if they're not there already) you'll find
us keeping ourselves to ourselves, only breeding if
the beech harvest is good, sleeping the northern
winters off, bingeing through good autumns.

Think of me as everymouse, whom the Romans ate
and the raindrop coshed, as I climbed and sprung the stalk
in fields where ploughs turn up pieces of pot;
Rome fell, but here my radius reaches out
to Luton, Leighton Buzzard, the green on the map,
the blur in the wing mirror, the hills from a train;
a conquest of the back gardens slow as money
taking root, as it does. I've noticed of late

the arrival of the dormouse box, and I'll take
to this like a stockade. So civilised.
Crawling out under a sky brilliant with stars
a few degrees out of whack, full of dead gods
and symbols I'll outlive, I feel a rush
pass through me, tip to tail, like the express
heading north, for what lies ahead, for whatever's past.
Before the night's hard work, I allow myself that.

W N HERBERT

A HEART OF TREES

In the big hills of Cumbria
cladded with mist
in that pale green you hate
before Penrith
I thought I saw
a heart of trees,
a cordial plantation
on the side of a hill
bare of leaves
growing through decades.

I'm almost sure
it wasn't planted
in that shape, with that gesture
but I take it as we pass Shap
in this train rushing back
to you, each tree
for a remembered embrace
its branches held up in witness
placing ring after ring
on your fingers.

JACOBITE'S LADDER

Once I dreamt that my head was a stone
shoved beneath a throne in London,
and that a troop of kings and queens
in progressively cleaner regalia
came and sat on my head
for a period of years,
breaking their royal wind into my ear.

As I lay stifled there, I saw
a ladder stretching from the top of the Law Hill
into the soup-flecked clouds,
and climbing up and down this blue ladder
were a series of patriots, some historical,
some fictional: all more real
than the town spluttering beneath them,
at least to the monarchs, who shifted
their faith-defending buttocks
uncomfortably throughout.

There were the renowned Pictish heroes:
Drost of the hundred battles; Brude,
son of Pontius Pilate; and Nechtan,
slayer of mere Northumbrians, all
wearing unknown costumes and recounting
unknowable legends. There were
the triumvirate of television, stage and screen:
Wallace, Bruce and Scottish Play, all
preceded by their faithful definite articles.
There were the terrible Caledonian twins: North
and the Shepherd, Burns and McGonagall,
Louis and Stevenson; and there
were the tribe of Trocchi, all
of whom drank of the waters of Leith and acquired
the powers of literary amnesia. That's right:
they didn't know they were born.

Then I was wrestling with Big Tam
dressed as a galley slave
and as we fought he whispered
the history of the golf ball in my other ear:
'Wooden, feathery, Haskell.'
And when he got to gutta-percha
I nutted him with my stony pow,
and as he fell he muttered,
'You'll never get to Marbella
with a shwing like that.'

Then I was the hammer of Mjollnir
driving spikes into the blue palms of the sky,
nailing a saltire of jet-trails into place
over Cambuslang. There was writing on
my temples, words cut into the stone,
but I found no one who could read them, nor
could I find a mirror, and yet I knew
these were my land's commandments.
When I awoke, I named the place
where I had rested 'Stonehaven'
and journeyed on my way rejoicing
beneath a great pyramid of cloud.

FOR ANDREW WATERHOUSE

For the good are always the merry
Save by an evil chance

                    W.B.Yeats, 'The Fiddler of Dooney'

An Irish reel is in my ears
            not one of yours;
Northumberland has rival airs,
but that was what they played
the night I heard: *The Sligo Maid* –
            strange what endures.

Displacement is our theme of themes,
            it's what remains:
the way we can't remember dreams
that still, like partial songs, affect
the unmelodic intellect
            and tune our brains.

So poets from the splintered North
            have made roots here:
from south of Humber, past the Forth,
come settler saplings slow to bear
the fruit and leaves that feed the air
            if granted years.

And that was what you couldn't give
            your own songs' book
the music's womb that wants to live
no matter what your mind may feel:
we write laments for all the reels
            that your hand took.

But what I mourn here more's the friend
    who died so friendless,
for no one could prevent that end
but you, displaced completely from
our love, your art - you needed numb-
    ness to be endless.

The fiddler's first above, says Yeats -
    let us abjure
all music past those pearl-stuck gates:
the breath inside a single air
is worth all heaven's atmosphere -
    yet can't endure.

COMRADE BEAR

Eh saw um sklent
               fae thi side o meh eh
medved at Sviblovo,
                  a bear on an escalator, amid
thi coats of airms, the letters
in anodised Church Slavonic aluminium.

Thi bear descendin thru thi platform
gangin doon wi nae murmel o sang
tae thi hinny belly core
                     cucurbit o sweet lava
wi thi glow pollen globes tae licht his wey
tae whaur thi blin bees
                  glammach an stir,
lady Cossack insecks wi thir spears
turning thi deid
               owre and owre
                     i thi glaizie glaur.

Eh saw thi bear descend tae glowr
at pharaohs and tsars
preservit in glycerine and tar
Triassic in aspic
               Jurassic in amber
borassic i thi braziers and mire.

medved (Медведь) - a bear.
sklent - sideways; *mermel* - murmur; *hinny* - honey; *glammach* - snap
at; *glaizie* - glittering, sleek; *glaur* - sticky mud; *borassic* - penniless.

METAPHOR FOR MALCHIK

Dogs don't use metaphor
                    Ruth Padel

I have been burying the delicious white stick.
I have been sniffing the butthole's brown flower.
I have caught the wooden wingbone:
here it is.

I have returned to the stomach's liquid child,
to the lumpy feast. I have been licking
my own soft chestnuts:
here they are.

Why do you tug the neck's strap-on tail
when this Volga of hot bitch-scent
has just poured past?
There she is.

I make a tripod fountain.
I puddle up to the gadget of my new ipoodle.
I cock a wood'll woo her:
here it is.

She is squatting mother to the fragrant slug.
I am not distracted by the magnetic North
South East and West Poles of wee wee:
but there they are.

She's like the leg of a Chekhovian aunt
I must embrace. She's like the trousers
of the garden invader, ripe for perforation.
So she is.

She's like the white hole in the black air
that sucks out howls. She's like the tendons
that tug the skeleton of the pack together. In fact,
here we are.

JOAN HEWITT

THREE POEMS OF ABSENCE

Poem for an estranged daughter

It should be exquisite
small enough to fit
inside a locket which you then keep
inside a drawer.

It should be pure
so that you choose to wear it
on days when you feel far from perfect,
less than sure.

Let its slight weight
against your throat compose you,
reminding you how much you're loved;
what love is for.

Vernal Song

for a daughter.

1.

I'm treating your absence as a guest
who doesn't mind my staying
in a nightdress all day long,

arranging and rearranging words
you may not read, trying
to fill your silence with a song.

2.

I dream you sit cross-legged on the floor.
You're speaking and I'm listening to your voice,

a river just released, which flows
towards and past me over rocks.

It slows each time you smile or frown.
Your back is to the wall and it's not clear

if you are in the dream by choice,
or cornered, talking your way out.

It is your birthday and the Equinox,
when summertime begins. Is that how you slipped in?

Sunshine falls upon your hands:
the light I won by altering the clocks.

I never understood how all that works.
How light won must also mean light lost.

The Empty Stanza

It must be swept clean, kept aired,
the window opened on a real or an imagined scene.
It scarcely matters if a boy slithers over snow
in dirty trainers, or an improbably violet sea
does the moon's bidding under the sun.
Three chairs, in case they all turn up at once,
and a table to be scrubbed along the grain.
Ignore the whisperings at the door, which had you fooled:
only the familiar living and the dead, ready
to slip in and make themselves at home.
This is reserved for the lost living and no-one else.
It must at all times be kept locked.
Now hope they come when you are there;
that you'll still recognise their knocks.

THE CATCH

for two female voices

A

Bring in your dead and find a seat.
Yes, place them by you on the floor.

You've wrapped them up so beautifully,
it almost seems a shame to take them out.

Canvas, sackcloth, coloured string, and rope!
Are they *industrial* staples in the green chenille?

A warning. The corpse that you've been carrying round
may not be the one that you expect.

That parent, sibling, lover may have been replaced
by someone you only wish were dead,

possibly someone breathing in this room.
And after the kind of work we've done on genograms,

it may be that ancestors turn up.
B, I was told you've left yours at reception.

It'll be safe. Might it be a good idea,though,
as you were the only one to vote against

unwrapping, to start where we left off,
with the dream you were so keen to share?

B

I'm at a deathbed in an unfamiliar room
The skin on her arms is cracked like bark,

but she's not old. Her eyes are full of-
I can't be sure-intent, or what might pass for love.

I feel her hands should hold me safe
and yet I know I have to carry her backwards

through the house. I lift her easily,
and we pass down corridors of empty mirrors,

a desk with an appointment book, stacks of chairs.
When I feel the cold air on my neck

and see our double shadow on the sunlit wall,
I know we've reached the garden, that we're safe.

Then she turns slippery, impossible to hold.
I'm struggling and I look down to find her eyes

are locked on mine: not grateful- knowing!
I realise that I've been caught, I've swallowed

her hook, and if I try to put her down,
my throat, not hers, will tear and bleed.

A

Thank you, B, for bringing us this far
on a journey which you evidently cannot make alone.

No-one said unwrapping would be easy.
Now which of you is willing to begin?

THE MAESTRO

It's you and that Charlie Gorse, heads
stuck up the chimney, coaxing down
the parrot you let out of the cage
for a bet on which way she would fly.
The bird's black as a crow and trembling
and Charlie says his wife will kill you both.
The bowl of water's your idea; but it's Charlie
who blow-dries the corpse and lays it
gently in the cage, begging you to stay
for one more drink, just till she gets home.

I'm wearing your stories. They're big.
They hang off my shoulders and trail
in my soup. I don't care that the smiles
of those who outlived you are polite, even sad.
It's Pansy Street, the cart-horse drops dead
and you ring the undertakers with measurements
for a casket. I'm ignoring the child who says
Boring – it's engraved on my brain.
I'm raising my glass. We will hear it again.

JOAN JOHNSTON

A BLUE PLAQUE – ABOVE A FRONT DOOR,
FOR MY GRANDMOTHER

Our Heritage: this heavy door
– its grain, brass keyhole,
letterbox – she polished
each Tuesday without fail
using scrim, elbowgrease,
cream from a tin.

(Visitor – note how easy it is
to find this house among so many.
From the end of the street
a small child could locate
the white doorstep, its brightness
her landmark).

POL IN HER COFFIN

She's done with waiting for no man
but Al. Al and all his dallying.
Done with all the one-last-chances,
the hanging-on-for-five-more-minutes
after work, in the cold, at the tram-stop.

She's finished with that
and look what he missed: Pol
all done up, her curls still girlish.

FATHERS OF THE EARLY 50s

We saw them on Sundays from our prams,
their faces framed by empty skies:

the breeze at their backs
they pushed us out,

one hand gripping the handle,
a Navy Cut in the other, directed

under the curved palm, held between thumb
and middle-finger tips. Protected

from changes in the weather we watched them
as they squinted ahead, and we looked out

at what had just passed: purple fireweed
growing up through broken brickwork,

all the new-laid lawns with tidy edges
they'd mow and trim when we got back,

the climbing roses they'd hold us up to.

THE OLD BUS SHELTER

It stands at the side of a quiet B road
– brickbuilt on the unmown verge
and darkened by hawthorn's overhang. Rooted
in dead-nettle, thistle-fringed, a dank sanctuary

where no-one waits, leaning on a carved
walking stick, his wife seated inside
wearing sensible shoes and a brown headscarf,
a country basket on her knee.

Long arms of dog rose and bramble
stir in the breeze, uselessly beckon
as the occasional car in which I'm travelling
approaches and passes without ever stopping,

stirs the tall grass, long stems of cow parsley
which bend to the wheels then straighten and settle,
resume their vigil for the overdue bus I always look for,
expect, any minute, in my rear-view mirror.

THE BURNING MAP

The credits are rolling. Mam lays aside
the Sunday crossword, the cardigan
she's always been knitting, and yawns.

Between crimson curtains sunlight slants
through the bay-window, warms one arm
of the red moquette sofa then the other;

takes all afternoon to slide over the carpet
in orange squares that stretch into diamonds,
climb the wall, spotlight the mirror, illuminate

the ballerina perfectly balanced *en pointe*
and framed in gilt against white anaglypta.
Occasional dust-motes glint and flare

while outside Dad continues
scraping years of gloss off the back door.
Under the blue flame of the hissing blowlamp

paint blisters burst and peel away
like the map at the start of *Bonanza*.

MICHAEL McCARTHY

THE LONG ROAD TO LONDON

It was the rusted tongs by the hearth and the jackdaw's nest in the chimney
and the bellows lying on the floor and the broken hasp on the window
and the ghosts of ghosts in the hall and the onions hung from the rafters
and the pair of pewter plates that blindly gaped from the dresser

It was the draught in the wooden stairs and the silences from the landing
and the cobwebbed beams of the roof and the musty smell from the chamber
and the blue tinge of the cheese and the crumbs on the big oak table
and the turnip rind on the floor and the rats running in from the stables

It was the creak of the rotting door and the sound of a horse and carriage
and the powder's purple smell and the reek of ale from the soldier
and the lantern's leaded lights and the way that his face looked swollen
and the wrought iron gate and the hedge and the long road to London.

THE FIELDS

Before Aunt Nora ever sent me that prayer book
with the red cover, before *St Albert the Great*
and *The man who got even with God*, before
school books and books from the Library Van
I was reading the fields and the run of the land.

The pathway that ran straight as a story
through the middle of the field below the house
coming to a full stop at the well. The pond
where the gander ruled and the geese hissed
the hill-field, and the meadow with the chained bull.

The brake, its folds dressed forever in yellow furze
with spiders hiding in their nylon webs. Pairc na Phurt,
the bog, the field where the rabbits sat on the rock
and the Camlach field, and the road that ran down
to the inches, to the river singing its own song.

The big inch where we learned to swim, the coarse inch
where we galloped the horse, the long inch where
the hares had their set and the flood came out,
and the spot where my father hid, up to his nose
after drowning the dog, the time of the Black and Tans.

The gravel field with the dug-out where they slept,
the briar field, Catherine's bog, Conaic na Muc,
Graif na Linnga, Claishe Ghapail, the fields by the road,
the field at the cross. The Moonaideen, Pairc na Bharrica,
the cabbage garden, and the field in front of the house.

Fields where cows grazed in summer then trudged home
weighed down with milk; where heifers stood stock-still
under trees, drizzle gathering like jewels on their backs.
The field where the fox jumped out through the ferns
brazen as the sky with a hen in his mouth.

Fields in spring where potato drills were lines on a page.
Autumn fields lyrical with oats, verses of barley in stooks.
Turnips in winter fields, exclamation marks on frozen ground.
They're all one field now, ditches a thing of the past.
Under my bare feet still the grammar of the grass.

COLD HILL POND

There are things it's not necessary to know.
The depth of the pond for instance. Who cares?
Its depth is upwards. The mirror it makes
Is what matters, and what that mirrors:

The movement of clouds. The wide canopy of trees
Before the leaves fall. The double breasted swan
Still as sadness, her domed wings rippled
Contemplative, the tips joined in prayer.

This pond is not for swimming. It's for seeing
What is in the sky and what is not in the sky:

The bales of straw, stacked and square
Like turrets of a Taj Mahal,
The peleton of Canada geese flying south,
Away from the blank cold, away from
The minus of things, to wherever
The swan imagines. I'm glad

It sits beside this twist of road
Each time I take the corner, too fast
For the fact of silence, for the depth of its
Imagining, for the slow heartbeat of the sun.

THE HOLLY FIELD

There was no holly in it much, though
there was a holly tree, if you could call it that.
An old stump of a thing half strangled with ivy,
the few scrawny branches with barely a leaf on them
and never any berries, not even at Christmas.

What there was, was a sycamore tree
with a fork low enough to climb up on.
You could hide in its leaves with their
five fingers, and pretend you weren't there.

You could make it into a horse or a sailing ship.
You'd gallop him off down the fields as far as
the river and after he had a fine long drink
you'd jump across without falling off.

You'd sail around the world and watch
the different countries as they went past,
and after you got back, you'd climb down
and run in home for a drink of thick milk
before your mother put it in a cake.

But the best thing about the holly field
was the corncrake. You'd hardly ever
see them because they hid in the high grass,
but they said 'corn-crake' all day long until
they got hoarse, and carried on long after
you were sent to bed while it was still bright.

When the time came for cutting the hay
they'd go all quiet. The horse pulled
the mowing blade up and down the field,
and when it came to the very last sward
they'd all fly out in a sudden whoosh
almost forgetting their legs. There was
no telling where they went next.

BEACHCOMBING

after George Mackay Brown

On day one a pair of dolphins appear. They swim parallel to the shore.
We watch each other then they are gone. I see them no more.

On day two I search the shingles and find a flat blue stone.
I skim it into the shimmer of waves; lose it in the sun.

On day three I sail out of Boston on board the Whaler Catalpa.
Our mission: the rescue of Fenian convicts off Freemantle.

On the fourth day a fine-figured blonde woman walks my way.
I see the skin of her neck is shrivelled, her face half eaten away.

On the fifth day a hermit crab crawls out of his shell.
In time he'll grow another. I'll have the original.

On day six at dawn a black woman walks out of the sea.
Says she is Queen Esther; she'll heal me under the medicine tree.

On day seven I read about scalping in Texas in 1849
A white horse rides by with pink fetlocks, blood-orange mane.

On the eighth day a waiter in Mickey Mouse gear says the food is good.
Five hundred percent better than yesterday. Guaranteed.

Sundown, day nine, the incessant sound of an African drum.
Prevent-us-from-error. Prevent-us-from-error. From-error. Amen.

SEAN O'BRIEN

READING STEVENS IN THE BATH

It is Newcastle at evening. It is far
From the furnished banks of the coaly Tyne
But close beside the hidden and infernal banks

Of the unutterable Ouseburn. Howay. It cries
Its native cry, this poisoned soup of prawns.
Howay. The evil river sings. The mind,

In Forest Hall, the haunted disbelieving suburb
Like a field of snowmen, the mind in Forest Hall
Lays by its knitting and considers

Going to the Fusilier. Howay. But in the upper room,
The room upstairs, the upstairs room,
The blear of glass and heat wherein

Not much is visible, a large pink man
Is reading Stevens in the bath. Howay. It is bath-time,
The time of the bath, the green-watered, where the mind

Lies unencumbered by the body as by time.
It is the bath as absolute, admitting
No conditional of green, the bath in which the bather

Lies considering. And the mind takes out
Its lightness to inspect, and finding nothing there
Begins to sing, embodying, emboldening its note.

It is the singing body in the bath, the mind.
Bookless Fruiterers, tell me if you can
What he may find to sing about, that man

Half-audible, and howling, as it were, the moon
That rests its gravity on weary Forest Hall,
That sends its tidal song by Tyne,

By Ouseburn, by the purifying plant
And ultimately here, to this balneum absolute,
Steam-punkah'd bath at the end of the mind, whose singer

Sings beyond the scope of tongues and sanity
Of neighbours, howling like a wolf among the snowmen
To the moon which does not listen:

Say it's only a paper moon,
Sailing over a cardboard sea,
But it wouldn't be make-believe

If you believed in me.
Howay. Howay. Howay!

INDIAN SUMMER

these iron comforts, reasonable taboos

John Ashbery

Look at this frosty red rose leaning over
The milk on the step. Please take it. But leave me
Its fragrance, its ice in the mind, to remember you by.
The girlfriends of afternoon drinkers
(O the criminal classes, their bottle-tanned lasses)
Have locked up their halters and shorts –
Being practical girls, they have understood soon
What I struggle with late, getting grit in my eyes –
That the piss-palace garden is windy and dim
When the heat goes at four. It is over again.
Now the engineer turns up to service the heating
And says: *I see your bell's still bust*
From the Charon-cold depths of his anorak hood.
The dark house is a coffin of laws; early closing.
But if the clocks must forever go back
To the meantime of Pluto, leave me your voice,
Its rumour at the confluence of Portugal and Spain,
From whose entwining waters rises, like a shell
Within the echo in the ear, your own supreme Creole.
If I am doomed to winter on the Campo Mediocrita
Whose high plateau becomes the windy shore
Of an ocean with only one side, to wait
Where the howling sunshine does not warm me,
Let me speak your tongue, at least –
For yours is the music the panther laments in,
Retreating to Burradon, yours is the silvery
Script of the spider at midnight,
Your diary is scandal's pleasure-ground
From which a bare instant of cleavage or leg
Is all I shall have to sustain me. And yours
Are the text and the age I should like to be acting:

You lie on the bed of the lawn, painted gold,
With the base of your spine left naked to breathe,
And now I might seal the extravagant promise
To kiss you to life with your name, if for once
You could look at me - do it now - straight
In the eye, without smiling or shaking your head.

BLIZZARD

The snow will bring the world indoors, the fall
That saves the Gulf Stream and the Greenland Shelf.
White abolitionist of maps and calendars,
Its Lenten rigour pillowed like a sin, it means
To be the only season, falling always on itself.
To put an end to all redundancy, pure cold
That proves what it need never say,
It calls us home again, beneath a drift
In which the figure and the ground collapse –
No more of metaphor, no more perhaps.

Look at these attic windowsills, look in the grate –
White after white against the off-white sheets,
The wafers of a pitiless communion
That turns a wood to Mother Russia and the night
To afterlife, then to a snowblind street.
With cataracts and snow-tipped breasts
The mermaids in their brazen lingerie
Wait bravely at the fountain in the square.
Green girls, they think it is their destiny
To offer the ideal to empty air.

Forgive me that I did not understand
That you were actual, not merely art,
That your fidelity was courage, that I failed
To honour you, to recognize your pain,
To grasp that snow once fallen will not fall again.
Now it grows clear: the world is not a place
But an occasion, first of sin and then the wish
That such self-knowledge may be gratified,
While snow continues falling, till we learn
There will be neither punishment nor grace.

ELEGY

Just round a corner of the afternoon,
Your novel there beside you on the bed,
Your spectacles to mark your place, the sea
Just so before the tide falls back,
Your face will still be stern with sleep

As though the sea itself must satisfy
A final test before the long detention ends
And you can let the backwash take you out.
The tall green waves have waited in the bay
Since first you saw the water as a child,
Your hand inside your father's hand, your dark eyes
Promising you heartbreak even then.
Get on with it, I hear you say. *We've got no choice.*

We left the nursing home your tired chair.
They stole the sweets and flowers anyway
And bagged your clothes like rubbish in the hall.
Here in the flat your boxed-up books and ornaments
Forget themselves, as you did at the end.
The post still comes. The state that failed to keep the faith
Pursues you for its money back. *There's nothing worse,*
You used to say, *than scratting after coppers.*
Tell that to the clerks who'd rob your grave,
Who have no reason to remember how
You taught the children of the poor for forty years
Because it was the decent thing to do.

It seems that history does not exist:
We must have dreamed the world you've vanished from.
This elegy's a metaphysical excuse,
A sick-note meant to keep you back
A little longer, though you have no need to hear
What I must say, because your life was yours,
Mysterious and prized, a yard, a universe away.

But let me do it honour and repay your gift of words.
I think of how you stared into the bonfire
As we stood feeding it with leaves
In the November fog of 1959,
You in your old green coat, me watching you
As you gazed in upon
Another life, a riverside address
And several rooms to call your own,
Where you could read and think, and watch
The barges slip their moorings on the tide,
Or sketch the willows on the further shore,
Then in the evening stroll through Hammersmith
To dances at the Palais. *Life enough*,
You might have said. *An elegant sufficiency*.
There was a book you always meant to write.

You turned aside and lit a cigarette.
The dark was in the orchard now, scarf-soaking fog
Among the fallen fruit. The house was far away,
One window lit, and soon we must go back
For the interrogation to begin,
The violence and sorrow of the facts
As my mad father sometimes dreamed they were
And made the little room no place at all
Until the fit was past and terrible remorse
Took hold, and this was all the life we had.

To make the best of things. Not to give up.
To be the counsellor of others when
Their husbands died or beat them. To go on.

I see you reading, unimpressed, relentless,
Gollancz crime, green Penguins, too exhausted
For the literature you loved, but holding on.
There was a book you always meant to write,
In London, where you always meant to live.

I'd rather stand, but thank you all the same, she said,
A woman on the bus to Hammersmith, to whom
I tried to give my seat, a woman of your age,
Your war, your work. We shared the view
Of willowed levels, water and the northern shore
You would have made your landing-place.
We haven't come this far to give up now.

IMMORTALS

Strathspey

At five the day begins a slow withdrawal
From the mountain valley and the silver roar
Of all its urgent streams. As dark comes on,
The sky and the snow in the forest
Are not grey but *gray*, American gray,
Like inbred Appalachian rebels
Lying where they fell beside the Bloody Brook.

Inside the lodge, it is too late for us.
We sit on in the library, surrounded
By the photographs of Eton OTCs,
And smoke-shadowed portraits of womenfolk
Shrivelled and crazed since they joined the firm.
All they have left are the hooks on their backs,
But we become invisible.

For this is home to a confederacy. Their dead
Will not lie down, not even for the afternoon.
They have to own the air along the corridors,
And in the dining-hall beneath the snow-gray dome,
And outside on the snow-covered terrace
Where wrought-iron tables and chairs provide
Both audience and cast for a Chekhovian promenade.

-Grandmother, when shall we see Edinburgh again?
-Not in my lifetime, child, and I shall never die,
Not while the world affords me lace and bombazine.
There is no other world but ours, and those
Unlike ourselves are only servants in disguise.
Slaves and cotton, sugar and rum,
Turn the globe till Kingdom Come.

JACOB POLLEY

MAN

Take up the carpets and apply weather
to the front door until it begrudges its frame.
Chip the gloss work, riddle the earth with stones –
let the tap spit out its washer.

Flaunt greasy ceilings and empty walls,
loosen floorboards and the bog seat,
block the sink, break the circuit,
have him make a necessity of six inch nails.

Grieve him to look deeply into the machine
and chronicle its black decline
in a rag with an already spotted history –
thistle the lawn, rot the tree.

Hail white wash, the improvement of echoes
by tiling, the burial of the dog,
the sundry Sundays of God-foreseen odd jobs
when your man might less-than-idly suppose

that he could drag open the great tool box,
descend its short flight of steps
and have them fold away over his head.

THE BYRE

There's a boy in the byre after dark, after school,
with his hands on the flanks of the beasts
as they breathe. And the coffin paths and drovers' roads
and yellow-lit farmyards stand utterly still.
The running waters with their overspill,
the woods and the wetlands: all wait.

Far off, the Princes' Streets and circuses,
the bypasses and contra-flows,
the crawler lanes, carriageways, viaducts and rails
groan with their masses and traffics and freights
while delis and arcades and paper shops glow,

and the boy in the byre after dark,
after school, listens to the breathing cattle
clatter on the byre floor, and knows
their heat as his, his presence as their peace
and their peace as his. The folded hills

are full of snow, the cars parked, the dogs in.
Far off, the cities grind on their axes
of orange light, while owls sweep the field's edge,
and old mines and caves of focused slate
crowd their dark around each drip as it drops.

Nothing stops, upland or low.
See who sleeps or serves, keeps or lets go,
herds or heals, builds or grows.
See the boy who brings his thoughts
to forget among the animals at nightfall –
how he leaves them quietened in the stalls.

GLOVES

Remember how you wore them in,
hands of your hands, how the leather
lined and cracked like aged skin?
Easy to lose, and whatever
good would one have been? But here,
creaturely and soft, they lie together,
one on top of the other:
I was rude to so suddenly
open the drawer and have them stop
tickling themselves and the dark.

We make the world no better
by putting it to use, and here
your empty hands, hands of air
that smell of oil of sweat, have for years
had none. No. Whose hands are ever
still, who lives with purpose,
making and using, doing and improving?

Today I took them out and tried them on.
My hands were too small and my fingers
in your fingers left room my fingers
will not fill. A loose glove profits
no man's hand. Once I put my hand
in yours, hand of my hand, hand
whose holding bettered me, and then let go.

EVICTION

Barefoot, they've entered the outermost place.
She covers her breasts. He hides his face.
Behind them stands the light-filled, grey stone, arched
city gate. The un-worked earth is parched.

Their shadows lag and elongate,
longing towards the shade. Everything waits
to be suffered, as now the garden's streams
and orchards lie, outside their lives, in dreams.

He howls into his hands. Her upturned forehead's
smooth and white; her mouth, though small, is wide.
They are, after all, only adequate,

and flesh, and grieve at the easily understood
threshold of grief, from where one, fully dressed
and armed, shoos them indifferently into the west.

LAST NIGHT

At the end, what we'll wish we'd done
more often, was lock in our noise
and books, pocketing the glimmer
of the key and then, while the glow
was still leaving our eyes and heaven
remained doubtful, depthless and un-starred,
walk into the live air under the trees
in dark from which an everyday hill
grew out of the world to allow
two to climb and sit, as if at the mouth
of a cave, and stare into the back
of time and memory, once and before,
reading in the rare ordinary night
their freedom to want for nothing more.

KATHARINE TOWERS

THE ART OF FUGUE

'Fugue must perform its…work with continuously shifting melodic fragments that remain in the "tune" sense perpetually unfinished.'
                                        Glenn Gould

The violins pronounce their notes with care,
as if they are a question.
The flutes concur and answer in shy voices.

This is a beautiful subject. It bears repeating
by more solemn instruments, which yawn
and clamber to their feet: yes, they suppose they feel the same.

There's a sudden clamour of delight
that things could be so simple:
the clean white sail of a tune making everything good.

If they could find a way to make an end,
they would do it now, using their own words.

PIANOLA

This is the tune it has known all along
but kept in its puppeteer's chest of velvet and string.

The notes of Chopin's *Ballade* march out,
as if years of practice have put them
beyond the reach of mistake or expression.
The keys dip and lift, efficient as clocks,

and we notice the piano's reluctance to tremble or weep
as the signature dims into minor. When the *adagio* comes
there's no sigh, no blissful easing of fingers,
only a rickety pause that wants to be over.

With the last chord, the piano relaxes and shudders,
as if it has said what it meant, and none of it mattered.

WEATHER

If we stand in woods after rain
when the trees are iron and purple
like wine, we'll put off our leaving –

not to wait for the woollen comfort of dusk
or to hear the wind flinching back
from the heart to let it be quiet and still

but to stand in the iron and purple
of evening, our stories behind us
like toys we've forgotten or lost

and enter at last the place in the heart
the place in the dark of the heart
where there's nothing, not even weather.

CHILDHOOD

These criss-cross lines printed on the snow
are bones of trees laid bare by the moon.
We should not be looking so hard

at what a tree would rather keep to itself.
Would we not fear to be shown
how like replicas we are, and how mechanical?

The joints and angles run across the field
complicating into knotty webs of twigs
no stronger than our fingers.

We could play that childhood game, stepping out
along the branches – pretending to teeter –
as if we still believed we couldn't fall.

THE GLASS PIANO

No, I did not swallow or inhale the glass piano;
it has grown inside me like a crystal in salt water

or an alien cell, accreting string after string and keys
until one day I reached the full eight octaves.

Inside where I should be soft plush I'm sharp,
my lungs a dark moth pinned by the piano's lid

while my heart keeps time to the keyboard's dip and lift.
Some days I'm loud: I growl bass chords

or sigh chromatically from A to middle C,
play a waltz or gigue and make notes hurtle from my skin.

Still I keep my distance; clasped or grasped I'll shatter
endlessly, describing all the themes and variations.

TONY WILLIAMS

POEM FOR TUESDAY

for James Sheard

Tuesday, you are waiting for me
just out of reach – further away than Monday,
of course, but nearer than the rest of next week.
Tuesday – with your full-tilt weekday clatter,
tendency to flash by regardless of deadlines,
and promise of dog-training classes in the evening.
Tuesday, the bank-holiday fall-back of all events
habitually scheduled for Mondays, except
the emptying of the bins, which seems to drag on
randomly across the whole of the following fortnight.
Tuesday, precursor of Wednesday with its awful
midweek finality – and rival of that day
for the transmission of European club football.
Tuesday, on which I used to have History
in the morning and English in the afternoon,
and by the time English was history I'd be
sure once again that I was in love with my English teacher
in spite of her grey hair and disciplinarian approach –
Tuesday, in whose early evenings
I ran home to masturbate joyfully
with the after-images of Miss Pearson
and Eustacia Vye fresh in my mind.
Tuesday, irreproachable day,
your morals and the sound of your name
are both sweet beyond measure. Who would have thought
you were named after the god of battle, or that he
would have his hand bitten off by an enormous wolf
and be cuckolded by a fish of mischief?
You, Tuesday, would never
commit fornication outside marriage.
Your modesty does you credit.
I imagine you as a vicar's daughter in a floral dress,

but don't let that put you off. Bread and butter of days.
Excellent day for appointments, harvest time at the desk,
Tuesday, you are truly one of the footsoldiers of Time
and your position in the ranks makes you likely to coincide often
with my gentler pleasures, such as a couple of pints
with a friend, providing the ambience is not blighted,
as it occasionally is under your auspices, by quiz night.
Tuesday, I roll grumpily into your mornings
without comment, O inferior cousin of the weekend
and day marginally to be preferred to drear Monday
and Friday-imitating Thursday. Tuesday,
the love of all the world's plain brown birds
and non-flowering grasses flows through you.
Wait in your tumbledown altar while I make
the remainder of my grand observances to Sunday,
your suzerain, and slouch through the grim duties
of the day that follows, your deathly leader
whose name I have mentioned
too many times already
for those worry-warts, the astronomers.
See you the day after tomorrow – may the sun
shine a little first thing in the morning
and then nothing all day, may your hours
fit together somehow into the regulation twenty-four
without anyone getting run over or the Gregorian calendar
falling suddenly into disuse, may my meeting with Jim
be as Tuesday,
be as amicable and restorative as ever.

LATE SCHOOLBOYS

The speed of their gallows walk's
lower even than their backpacks,
slung pained and aslant like their
dissenting grimaces. Trudging, more

stop than start, they take long-cuts
in twos and threes through the drab bits
of scrub tacked on to public parks,
meet the dogs on their walks

and their stoic, indifferent owners. Some
lost glove rots in front of them
all winter, and they know each flake
of paint on the railings their sticks rattle.

They'll arrive in a ragged parade
that mourns into the school's facade
and wait for the worst to burst over them
in a spat shower of opprobrium.

The birch, the worn footpath's line,
the pavements and tarmac patches they learn
over years of yawns and missed breakfasts,
the dread of the official lists,

are not on the syllabus;
nothing that interests them is.
They know only the equation of day
and death, and they avoid it stubbornly,

rolling over on their lives
and bright futures as depressives.
They have their love affairs with sleep
and blush at Miss. They speak in burps.

Lateness is the state of grace
they travel through and in this place
where their dazed craniums
conceive the codas of their dreams

they daub their uniforms with mud
to make the powers storm and chide
and have confirmed that everyone
despises them, and they the sun.

LISTENING

I didn't mean to overhear
the scrape of chair legs on the floor
and sour breath of the bored, enshadowed janitor
nor how he conflabbed on the stairs
(it echoed in the squarish well)
with an ingrate from HR, how you
were falling basementwards, towards
the ferret-sprainted woods where mats
of needles are being disturbed and skulls
of foxes, badgers, falcons, bats and shrews
emerge like eggshells of the news.
I heard the round of sirens in the night,
the airless click of satellites.
I heard the muffle and the timely knock,
the seconds jerking round the clock,
lonely and insomniac,
the sound of no one coming back
to fill and free the lock. I heard
a drunk man shouting COCK
and shrunken voices answering No,
his loiter in the orange yard
and how he turned to go
against a wind that breathed your name.
I heard the water cooler's hiccup send
a bubble of the future up,
an iciness to be my friend,
and how beyond the traffic's burr
your cough performed a Pyrenees of grief
upon a screen – as I was dropping off – I heard,
between the dog barks and the Word of God,
a vixen's scalp-contracting scream.
I heard the silence of the room.
I saw the silence of the moon.

THE CORNER OF ARUNDEL LANE
AND CHARLES STREET

Midwest tornado-hunters do not storm
    across the desert with more warmth
than I, attracted by the sunset's flare,
    fly to where it sinks, and stare
tender and dispassionate as a friend
    at what is coming to an end,
the evening of a dormant farm, or house
    untenanted and verminous.
I travel randomly by foot and bus,
    and with no data from the skies
to guide me to the gruesome, mossy yard
    by which my atmosphere is stirred,
the gulf of house-backs, broken pots and drains
    which no whole window looks upon;
like them, to satisfy my human lust
    for seeing things reduced to dust
and have my sadnesses provoked, I race
    towards the funerals of place,
and watch – and watching feel myself grow rich –
    the infill of a stagnant ditch,
then find a dirty pub and hold a wake,
    alone, and toast the world's mistake.
My fellow guests wear suits of soot. We speak
    about the state their crumbling brick
betrays. Their chimneys are forlorn salutes
    to something going down the chutes.
I thank the curve of their decline that makes
    their final moment mine. I take
the back way through the England-flagged estate,
    shin up and leap a padlocked gate
and cross the paddock where no horses are,
    the yellow grass, where I inter

the moment of the dying of the dead,
    and I am turning in the road
to catch its final flash of sun, its gasp
    of clarities. If you should pass
a *Private* sign by ivy-covered cliffs
    inside a fly-tipped wood, and if
a culvert empties at its foot into
    a runnel, canalized and blue
with algae, petrol and pollutant scum –
    then call me, tell me, and I'll come
and duck the wire, stand on the concrete foot-
    bridge, fondle the freezing rail and put
a cough of benediction on the blight
    that takes its time upon the site,
for what that's worth. And when I come to die
    deserted pavements, streets, will sigh,
an iron set of steps will ring and chime,
    pretending that it knows my name,
atonal effigies of hymns to praise
    the rain, and Nowhere breaking loose.

RECKONING

You think you're metal and I think you're mental,
You think you're lintel and I think you're lentil,
You think you're freehold and I think you're rental,
But what does it matter to either of us?

You think you're amble and I think you're stumble,
You think you're treble and I think you're trouble,
You think excitable, I think unstable,
But what does it matter to either of us?

You think you're cello and I think you're callow,
You think you're open and I think you're hollow,
You think of yesterday, I of tomorrow,
But what does it matter to either of us?

You think you're pizza and I think you're pasta,
You think you're faster and I think you're fester,
You think you're Lisbon and I think you're Leicester,
But what does it matter to either of us?

You think you're winkle and I think you're cockle,
You think you're heckle and I think you're hockle,
You think a torrent and I think a trickle,
But what does it matter to either of us?

But what does it matter, but what does it matter,
But what does it matter to either of us?
But what does it matter, but what does it matter,
But what does it matter to either of us?

BIOGRAPHICAL NOTES

Peter Armstrong lives in Tynedale and is director of training at the Newcastle Cognitive Behavioural Therapy Centre. He was awarded an Eric Gregory prize in 1984. His publications include *Risings* (1988); *The Red Funnelled Boat* (1998); *The Capital of Nowhere* (2003) and a pamphlet, *Madame Noire* (2012).

Peter Bennet was born in 1942. He taught in schools then was tutor-organiser for the Workers' Educational Association in Northumberland. He has been a prizewinner in several competitions, including the National Poetry Competition, and one of his six collections, *The Glass Swarm*, was shortlisted for the 2008 TS Eliot Prize.

Colette Bryce's most recent collection of three is *Self-Portrait in the Dark* (2008). Her books have received several awards, including the Aldeburgh Prize and the Strong Award, and individual poems have won the National Poetry Competition (2003) and the Academi Cardiff International (2007). She received a Cholmondeley Award in 2010.

Alistair Elliot was born in Liverpool in 1932 but has lived the better part of his life in Newcastle. He is a classicist and retired librarian. His two most recent books were *The Real Poems* (2008) and a reconstruction from fragments of Euripides' play *Phaethon* (2008).

Helen Farish lives in Cumbria and teaches at Lancaster University. She was Poet in Residence at the Wordsworth Trust 2003-4. Her first collection *Intimates* (2005) won the Forward Prize for Best First Collection and was short-listed for the TS Eliot prize. A second collection will be published in 2012.

Paul Farley was born in Liverpool and is Professor of Poetry at Lancaster University. The most recent of his three collections is *Tramp in Flames* (2006). Awards for his books include a Somerset Maugham Award, a Forward Prize for Best First Collection and another for Best Individual Poem, and the Whitbread Poetry Award.

W N Herbert was born in Dundee, lives in North Shields and is Professor of Poetry and Creative Writing at Newcastle University. The most recent of his seven collections, *Bad Shaman Blues* (2006), was a PBS Recommendation and shortlisted for the TS Eliot Prize.

New poems were published in *Three Men on the Metro* (2009).

Joan Hewitt was born in Liverpool and lives in Tynemouth. Her collection *Missing the Eclipse* was published in 2008. Poems have appeared in anthologies including *The Body and the Book*; *Not a Muse* and *100 Island Poems of Great Britain and Ireland*. In 2003 she was given the Northern Promise Poetry Award.

Joan Johnston was born and lives in Newcastle upon Tyne. She teaches writing in a wide range of community settings. In 2001 she received a Hawthornden Fellowship. Her collections include *Orange for the Sun* (2005) and *The Daredevil: Scenes from a Bigamist Marriage... and other poems* (2011).

Michael McCarthy, a native of West Cork, is a priest and spiritual director who lives in North Yorkshire. 'The Fields' won the Leslie Richardson Award; his first collection, *Birds' Nests and Other Poems* (2003), the Patrick Kavanagh Award and his second, *At the Races* (2009), the Poetry Business Book and Pamphlet Competition.

Sean O'Brien grew up in Hull, lives in Newcastle and is Professor of Creative Writing at Newcastle University. His first six collections won awards, including, for *The Drowned Book*, the 2007 Forward and TS Eliot Prizes. His latest collection, *November*, was shortlisted for the 2011 TS Eliot Prize, Forward Prize and Costa Poetry Award.

Jacob Polley was born in Carlisle, lives in Fife and teaches at St Andrews. He received an Eric Gregory Award and the BBC Radio 4/Arts Council 'First Verse' Award. His first collection, *The Brink* (2003) was shortlisted for the TS Eliot and John Llewellyn Rhys Prizes. He was Arts Queensland's 2011 poet-in-residence.

Katharine Towers was born in London and lives in the Peak District. Her first collection, *The Floating Man*, (2010), won the Seamus Heaney Centre Prize for Poetry, was a PBS Recommendation and was shortlisted for the Aldeburgh First Collection Prize and the Ted Hughes Award.

Tony Williams was born in Matlock, lives in Alnwick and teaches creative writing at Northumbria University. His first collection *The Corner of Arundel Lane and Charles Street* (2009) was shortlisted for the Aldeburgh First Collection Prize and the Portico Prize. A pamphlet *All the Rooms of Uncle's Head* was published in 2011.